Advanced Praise for *The Art of Perpetuation*

Alison Powell's *The Art of Perpetuation* is a Mobius strip of macro and micro that remakes the *Oxford English Dictionary* into a murder mystery and organizes the kaleidoscope of the natural world into an occult circuit board. In these pages, we encounter the archeological Red Lady who wasn't one at all, the dreaming Elon Musk and his Ray Bradbury cloak of sci-fi improbability, and the reverend geologist who ate the heart of Louis XIV and declared that he, "like all men of science, know[s] the body because of women and criminals." Powell is a wizard of history and metaphorical precision, and imbues her elusive subjects with unsettling magnetism, whether it's Aristotle arguing that the city is organic, "which is like saying cruelty is organic," or her compelling high school bully, who lives in her brain "and sparkles with her violence," much like these dazzling, prismatic lyric essays.

—**Simeon Berry, author of** *Ampersand Revisited* **and** *Monograph*

The Art of Perpetuation is an extended meditation that considers the slipperiness of images. From the archives of dolls to Louis XIV's preserved heart to personal memories, which are merely images embedded in the psyche, the reader is gifted with a contemplative poetic. This book interrogates how histories, persons, places, and things slowly fade from our present view and leave in their stead wonder, awe, human connection, identitarian query, or ontological mystery. Powell shows us the mind of a scholar, maker, and thinker who can simultaneously hold the answers and the questions. This is writing at its best and most compelling. *The Art of Perpetuation* is a book any writer worth their words will read and wish they wrote.

—**Airea D. Matthews, author of** *Simulacra*

THE ART OF PERPETUATION

LYRIC ESSAYS

Alison Powell

Black
Lawrence
Press

Black Lawrence Press

www.blacklawrence.com

Executive Editor: Diane Goettel
Chapbook Editor: Kit Frick
Book and Cover Design: Amy Freels
Cover Art: Yellow Sweet Clover, *Melilotus officinalis*, from the series "Exotic/ Invasive Species"
and Glossy Buckthorn, *Rhamnus frangula*, from the series "Exotic/ Invasive Species" by David
O'Neil Lambert. Used with permission.

Published 2020 by Black Lawrence Press.
Printed in the United States.

CONTENTS

NICE WANTON

"The monster a child knows best and is most concerned with
is the monster he feels or fears himself to be."

—Bruno Bettelheim

In a film titled *Lars and the Real Girl*, a man orders a life-size doll from a sex
toy company. He falls in love with it, names it, carries it to work and the
library, takes it out to dinner. After initial confusion and anxiety, the
townspeople adapt to the presence of the doll, who he has named Bianca:
bedroom communities know what to do with a neighbor like this, how to
fold him in and soften the sharp edges of his eccentricity. He has a child's
mind, the neighbors say to each other, observing his awkward, inward
mannerisms. He has the stutter of a shy nine-year-old. He is like a girl
with a doll, not a man with a sex toy. The neighbors begin to talk to the
doll like she's real, taking on his fantasy as parents indulge children by
pretending to feed or sing a lullaby to a stuffed animal. By the film's end,
Bianca disappears like a pair of crutches that magically fall apart just as
the invalid takes his first steps. She was a practice girl, a rubber-bodied
training bike. A man can use a doll as a type of practice dummy for a
real woman; conversely, a real woman can be a type of doll, though it is
doubtless a rarer phenomenon.

———

Though dolls may seem to be tangible, idealized versions of women,
they lack the worldly things that make a woman frightening: a beating
heart, a unique moral outlook, a mouth that speaks. A doll, in its silence,

is sometimes worshiped. In Exodus when Moses left to collect the ten commandments, his brother Aaron gathered the gold earrings and gold ornaments of the Israelites, melted them, and shaped the cooling gold into a calf. When the Israelites responded with exultation, he built an altar before it to work, play, and pray around. Returning from Mount Sinai, Moses threw two Tablets of Stone at the golden calf before destroying it, grinding the gold into a powder to be mixed with water, which he forced the Israelites to drink.

The source of his rage was their violation of the second commandment, "Thou shalt not make unto thee any graven image ... for I ... am a jealous God" (Exodus 20.4-6), generally understood to be a statement against idolatry. Yet the rejection of idols by the apostles was arguably less because of the attachment humans might form to those objects and more about the materialism implied in such an attachment and the infectious quality of the object; as Psalm 115:8 reads, "They that make them are like unto them; so is every one that trusteth in them." That is, those who make idols are themselves unseeing, unfeeling, deaf to God's truth.

The man who loves the doll never risks becoming the doll himself. And whereas an idol can enrage a jealous God, dolls are valued precisely because of their divine passivity, the extent to which they can be manipulated. They can be staged in a tableau vivant—a dance, a tea party, a date—whereas an idol is rarely, if ever, poseable. Though dolls are traditionally silent, a contemporary doll can be, in the parlance of the trade, "a crier," a coveted feature in the most enthusiastically marketed dolls. An idol that cries is decidedly less festive. (Interestingly, the few statues that reportedly do so tend to have a female form, like that of the Blessed Virgin.)

Etymologically speaking, "doll" does not come from "idol," as one might expect. The word has its origins in Dorothy, a nickname which implied "plaything" and was given to loose women in the Renaissance. In a youth morality play called *Nice Wanton* from the mid-sixteenth century, a character by the name of Dalilah shames her brother for his taste in women, saying "ich tell your minion doll, by Gog's body: It skilleth not she doth hold you as much," meaning his girlfriend has cuckolded him (or as she says, has "putteth a bone in your hood").

The origin of the word "doll," then, lies in sexual deviance. Indeed, some of the earliest references to "doll" include it as a *dildoll* or form of dildo. In 1715 an author observed that "every day in St. James's Park women carry baskets full of dolls bought by young women of all conditions. When one lifts the doll's skirt, instead of legs is found a fabric-covered cylinder about 6 inches long and an inch in diameter."

——

The carving of idols tends toward the crude: they are typically made of hard material like metal, wood, stone, gold, or silver, lacking the subtle hand apparent in the Tickletoes, Rub-a-Dub Dolly, or Jody-an-Old-Fashioned-Girl dolls. The latter even has painted-on eyelashes. A brief dive into the world of dollmaking reveals the symphony of choices available to an ambitious dollmaker. A doll can be marked by its maker or not. Its body can be articulated, or pin-jointed, and made of cloth, plastic, vinyl, stuffed latex, kidskin, or a combination. It might be a Bent Knee Walker or have a Bent Limb Body. Its hair might be made of mohair, rooted or not, or molded plastic, or covered with a bonnet; it may have a pouty or watermelon mouth, a treble tongue. It could be a breather, with open or pierced nostrils; its eyes might be non-flirty or flirty, intaglio, weighted, fixed, sleeping, blown glass, decal, or pupiless.

One might also fall down a rabbit hole learning the provenance and names of such dolls, such as the Fate Lade, a fortune telling doll; the Frozen Charlotte or Frozen Charlie, a one-piece all bisque doll; or the Topsy Turvy, two dolls in one when you turn it over. The Trilby is multi-faced, and when you turn a knob on top of its head, the face changes: suddenly your Trilby is sleeping, smiling, crying, or has become a doll of a different race. The Little Wingy has dimples and a face coated with phosphorescent paint that glows in the dark, and the Posie Walker comes with bent knees that allow her to fully genuflect.

If an idol were to talk, it would doubtless be a recitation of scripture; when a doll talks, it offers a different sacred text, one that is obsequious and self-effacing, mischievous in the most saccharine way, as with the 1987 Worlds of Wonder Talking Julie doll:

Would you like to learn my secret words now? I'll say some words, and you say
them back to me. Okay? Okay. I make believe when I pretend. Say "pretend."
Okay. "Hungry" is one of my secret words. Say "hungry." Okay. Another word
for "song" is "melody." Say "melody." Okay. You can tell me to be quiet. Say
"be quiet." Okay.

Mattell's Charmin' Chatty, which has a narrow face and turned up nose
like a plastic Elizabeth Warren, has a tiny phonograph record player the
size of an Oreo cookie in her stomach that plays if you pull a white string
hanging between her shoulder blades. One can purchase records for this
player with titles like: *Scary/Animal Noises, Mother/Ridiculous, Good/Famous.* In
television ads, Chatty's phrases terminate exclusively with question or
exclamation marks:

I love you! Take me with you! Let's play house! Let's talk and talk! Would you
like pickle ice cream? What would you like to do? I just loooovvvee monsters!
I'm a donkey! Hee-haw! Let's have a party! I trust you! You're my friend! Are
we going somewhere? Are we making too much noise?

———

When my grandmother Marie died, my mother and I discovered her walk-
in closet to be full of clothes with store tags still on them. That closet
opened onto another, smaller closet, like a life-size jewelry box. I thought
of *Overboard*, when a working-class Kurt Russell builds a walk-in closet
complete with spinning shelves for the insufferable wealthy woman played
by Goldie Hawn. This smaller second closet was lined with dolls she'd
collected throughout her later life, most via international cruises she took
with her second husband who was a pharmaceutical rep for Searle, inven-
tor of NutraSweet and the birth control pill. They'd make those short
stops in another land, just long enough to snap a photo and pick up a local
souvenir. On white wire shelves the dolls stood upright on their stands,
international, intergenerational, old and new. There were porcelain
dolls, dolls with real hair, painted cheeks, bow-tie smiles, wearing the
stereotypical costumes of their local lands: the Spanish dancer in the red
and black lace dress, Dutch dolls with their wooden shoes. Many wore an

expression eerily similar to my grandmother: hospitable, cheerful, even, but a little bit blank and slightly surprised.

I don't know if my grandmother had a doll at all growing up, but it seems unlikely—maybe a corn husk doll like the kind you can get at the state fair. My grandmother was raised on a rural farm during the Depression along with eight brothers and sisters. As an adult she had the bare-faced, jovial consumerism of someone who came from significant poverty only to find themselves having married well, as if by accident. Her attitude toward life was in keeping with the poet Anatole France's statement that he "preferred the folly of enthusiasm to the indifference of wisdom."

One popular doll during her childhood was the poupee, or boudoir doll, made in the likeness of theatre actresses. With the short hair and flapper dress of the Gilded Age's "New Woman," the dolls signaled sexual and economic freedom. This worried, among others, Anatole France, who speculated the French birth rate was in decline because, in attending so tenderly to their boudoir dolls, women were forgetting their obligations. Max Schlapp, professor of Neuropathology, wrote at the time: "these exaggerated dolls are the temporary whim of abnormal women. I use the word advisedly, because women who are normal have children and have no time to waste on baubles."

Not all dolls are baubles, though; people make do with what they have. My great-grandmother Safrona—Marie's mother-in-law—was a farmer who raised chickens and dressed them for sale. She'd take the feathers off, cut off the feet, and clean them out. Then she'd give my mother and aunt the feet, showing them how to pull the tendons so they moved like a puppet. Safrona once gave my aunt a Christmas ornament made from a real wishbone wearing, bizarrely, a pink sweater she'd crocheted for it herself.

Many summers as a child I traveled to my grandmother's house in Louisville, Kentucky to stay for a week or so. The house smelled of her strong perfume and had a living room that was never used with white plush carpet and a shuffleboard table in the basement that was sprinkled with gritty sand. I looked forward to the pebbled gray cosmetics box my grandmother would put in my room. It contained ten or so Barbies made in the 1960s, most fully made up with hard, coarse hair set as tight as their mouths. The metal clasp opened with a satisfying, hard snap to reveal dozens of outfits and various accessories, some of which I still have—a sheer lace dress with dots, a blue cotton sundress, a white envelope purse with a tiny pearl button closure. Eventually the outfits became multi-era as I mixed in the Barbie clothes from my 80s youth—a glittery multi-colored pantsuit, a pink bubble sweater.

In *Overboard* Goldie Hawn's character Joanna loses her memory in a boating accident and is kidnapped by Kurt Russell, who gives her the name Annie and takes her to a rural shack, saying she is the mother of his three grubby, hillbilly children. In one scene she slumps over, slack, in a rocking chair while the children lob grapes at her face. Kurt Russell leans over and waves his hand before her glassy eyes, shouting cheerfully, "Hey! Baby doll! What's for dinner?" Eventually he carries her from the room while one son asks: "Dad. Can we trade her in for a new one?" When Annie finally speaks, she says to Russell, in a perfect upper-class East Coast accent, "My life is like death. My children are the spawn of hell, and you're the devil."

My grandmother never said an unkind word about her children or grandchildren. In fact, my mother said her mother was too kind to be trusted; as a girl she aligned herself with Safrona, who was cool-headed and tough at cards. Marie eventually moved to Florida with the pharmaceutical rep. Her body curled in on itself toward her final months; without a full-time nurse, she sat, dazed, on the living room couch listening to Fox News turned up to the highest volume. She ate cherry pie with a spoon, drank white wine, and shuffled out to the porch occasionally for a Virginia Slim. Toward the end her whole body took on the trembling of the elderly and she vibrated as if on a high wire, or like a bristle doll, that ancient Chinese doll made of silk and straw that dances on a copper plate when it's hit with a soft mallet. She had a nervous habit of smiling and then stopping the smile abruptly into a sudden grimace. The corners of her mouth would jolt upward and down, again and again. When I visited, we'd sit on the screened-in patio in the heat and she'd pat my knee and unwrap candy after candy, cellophane wrappers falling to the floor like little pieces of colored glass.

———

"You're never too old to play with dolls. Until you're DEAD."

—movie poster for *Dolls* (1987)

Most dolls exist on a continuum of sexiness that becomes apparent to children in tandem with their own maturation. As a child I was partial to androgynous, innocuous dolls: Strawberry Shortcake, Cabbage Patch, the generic small dolls that came with a dollhouse my mother won at the Indiana State Fair. My brother, six years older, was adept at finding small humiliations to weave throughout my day; he'd pose the figures from my dollhouse in awkward sex positions, legs and arms akimbo, atop the beige shingled roof. One afternoon he lined up my Cabbage Patch dolls on my bed with their pants pulled down, mooning whoever walked in the door. Though I remember my parents and brother chuckling at the prank, I was troubled by the ease with which the dolls were manipulated into such an unfamiliar pose. Suddenly they appeared to me to be floppy and insubstantial, vaguely complicit in their own defamation.

Mooning was big in the 80s. That same year his friend Jeremy mooned me—on a dare, I think—and this is my first memory of being shocked at nakedness. He stood in the end of our hallway, bent over with his bare ass in the air, and my parents sent him home early. Right around this time the horror movie *Dolls* came out, which I watched for the first time at a friend's sleepover. In the film, a handful of unrelated tourists end up at an old Victorian-style house in the woods run by an elderly dollmaker and his wife. They have an impressive collection of antique toys and, as it turns out, they are witches who punish immoral or transgressive guests by sending the toys to kill them. The guests are then made into dolls and become the ones to discipline future guests.

Two characters, Isabel and Enid, are the focus of the film's opening scene: their car has stalled and they're trying to hitchhike a ride. They stumble through a dense thicket dressed like *Who's That Girl?*-era Madonnas, laughing and obviously drunk. Their rambunctious energy is in stark contrast to the little girl we see in the film's next scene. Her pigtails are tied up in pink ribbons, and she's reading a book in the backseat of a car, obviously a good girl. By the end, Isabel, having tried to steal some antiques (calling them, memorably, "anti-queues"), has had her head bashed in by feminine dolls dressed in pink and lace; Enid searches for her only to find herself in front of a tiny army of toy soldiers who raise their guns and riddle her with bullets. The wicked stepmother of the good girl, who has humiliated and rejected her throughout the film, is stabbed by tiny toy knives until she leaps screaming and bloody out a nearby window.

And yet there is something sympathetic about the elegant, thin patriarch dollmaker of the house. When the guests sit around a dinner table for the first meal, he explains, surly, "No one wants a doll that's special anymore ... that's one of a kind." In the film, capitalism becomes linked to femininity; the little girls don't want his dolls anymore, so his boutique objects begin to embody his feeling of having been left behind. Each murderous doll has in its sights the tourists, the guests who don't intend to stay. When the stepmother asks him about his work ("What kind of work is that? Witch-craft?") the old man and his Red-Riding-Hood-grandmother wife laugh uproariously. Because what man is a witch? A man is a *maker*.

—

I like to sleep with you. I like to sleep with you. Is anyone else awake? Hold me close and whisper. I want to tell you something. I know a secret, do you? Will you tell me a story? Let's whisper—psst psst psst. My name is Baby Secret.

Darwin studied his children's behavior carefully, keeping fastidious notes, and so we know he took their wariness of nonhuman things with human features as a sign of their growing awareness and intelligence: "29v. March 1st 1842—A few days ago Emma gave her [a] doll, but she sensibly shuddered, when it was brought near her & would not for some days touch it." I would like Darwin, scholar of that uncanny valley of mat-ing rituals, to meet iDollators, people who are attracted to, and publicly partner with, life-size sex dolls. Darwin may have indeed been familiar with the concept. One tends to think of this as a contemporary phenom-enon, but it is hardly that; in *Adollizing; or, A Lively Picture of Adoll-Worship: A Poem in Five Cantos* (1748), the protagonist makes "a Doll, by new mechanic aid, As big as life," with which he engages in "frequent Adoll-worship," clearly intended as a reference to sexual activity.

The eccentric darlings of Internet sex communities, iDollators have established themselves on chat boards, Reddit accounts, and more, activity that has in turn resulted in magazine articles and documentaries. While there are, publicly at least, a handful of female iDollators, the vast majority are men. (When asked why, one man notes that the life-size silicone dolls are incredibly heavy to lift.) One iDollator activist, Davecat, is a Detroit area resident who lives with his dolls Sidore, his wife, and Elena, their girlfriend. Each of his "Synthetiks," as Davecat calls them, is expensive and made to order. Neither can, by herself, walk; in this, the dolls are not as advanced as the AutoPeriptekos, a wind-up Victorian doll I saw in a glass case in the London Museum of Childhood. But they also can't be, Davecat says, overly critical, unpleasant, or unfaithful. In interviews he moves effortlessly between reality and the realness of fantasy. He acknowledges Sidore doesn't eat; she lacks, as he says, a digestive tract. Yet he lists her favorite foods. Both dolls have a backstory: Sidore is the daughter of a Japanese father and English mother, and Elena was raised in Russia.

When Davecat describes being rejected by women, he uses the terms of capitalism, of competition and efficiency: once he was seeing "an organic lass," which worked for some months until she began dodging him after work. "I was beating myself up over it when I realized: Why am I wasting my time ... when I have a Doll who is in love with me at home? Plus ... I'm not competitive, either. I decided that pursuing her was a wasted effort."

Sidore, Davecat's wife, doesn't age, at least in the usual sense. Her first body lasted three years; the next, seven. Sidore's synthetic flexibility morphs into divine cooperativeness: besides being literally flexible, she is bisexual and polyamorous. He'd like to purchase more dolls but is of modest means—and no matter what, Dave adds with urgency, "Sidore will always remain my wife."

———

There are at least two documented cases of organic humans attempting to transform themselves through surgery into life-size dolls. One is Justin

Jedlica, known as "America's 'Ken Doll,'" who has had 140 surgeries in the past fifteen years. By 2012 he'd undergone rhinoplasty; chest, shoulder, bicep, thigh, tricep, and calf implants; brow shaving and lifts; cheek and lip augmentations; and gluteoplasty. Originally from Poughkeepsie, Justin and his partner now reside in their own Dreamhouse, Trump Tower.

In "Meet the Human Barbie" published in *GQ*, a reporter travels to Odessa to meet with the world's first "living Barbie" who goes by "Amatue." The article includes a large photo of what appears to be a Barbie doll perched awkwardly in the ocean, *Sports Illustrated* style; terrifyingly, the caption reveals her to be not a doll at all. Amatue's look is bizarre. According to the interviewer, any change in her facial expression happens only in her eyes, the rest of her staying unchanged; her waist, he writes with vivid brutality, is "basically a sock of skin around her spinal cord." On an all-liquid diet, Amatue sips carrot juice and mint chutney through a straw throughout the interview. She says her nails—a complex design made of tiny dots—came to her in a dream, as did her name. Everywhere she goes, she brings a chaperone, a Skipper of sorts named Olga who sports a self-designed purple Power Ranger outfit.

———

Let's pretend. You be the mommy, I'll be the little girl. Do you want to keep doing this?

I spent much of fourth grade with my best friend Kelli in a florescent-lit room in her basement. Once a laundry room, it was taken up nearly entirely by a large, manufactured wood desk, some nondescript cardboard boxes, and a massive Barbie Dreamhouse. We played there for hours, making up all kinds of dramas, the details of which mostly elude me, though I have a vivid memory of staring, vaguely frustrated, at Ken's inoffensive underwear—plastic ridges hiding, mysteriously, whatever lay underneath.

Kelli had long brown hair tied with thick yarn-like ribbons. Upon entering her house, a nondescript split-level ranch on a cul-de-sac, I'd often be nearly felled by a miniature Schnauzer, an excitable gray ball of muscle. I knew Kelli was too nice a girl for me, though she once hosted a sleepover that included a game where each person left the room one at a time, so the remaining girls could discuss, and later articulate to her, the missing girl's worst qualities. I craved approval from Kelli and her family; their pliable hospitality differed from the irritable authenticity of my own. They went to church and didn't say unkind words in public. They were always wearing that wide American television smile.

Kelli's mother had a sort of romantic, if weird, glamour. At school some kids said that Kelli's mother was nuts, because though it was the 1980s, she maintained a decidedly 1960s kind of look. Some vintage looks are translatable to subsequent eras, but hers was not: she wore her brunette hair in twin buns on either side of her head like Princess Leia, and her makeup included comically round circles of bronzer, bruise-blue eyeshadow, and frosted pink lipstick. She *always* looked like this, even wearing a late 60s housecoat in the morning in the middle of winter after a night of making us chocolate-dipped marshmallows.

One summer I stayed with Kelli at her cousin Sarah's house in the middle of the countryside. Sarah's mother was a lightly subversive, short-haired single working mom who let us sleep in her bed at night because it was the only room with a window AC unit. Behind the house were rows of orchards, none of which belonged to her. One morning Sarah and I got up early and microwaved pancakes, and after we'd finished rehearsing our dance routine to Debbie Gibson's "Out of the Blue," Sarah told me Kelli's mother dressed like that because her husband had had an affair. She'd seen them together in the Kroger parking lot; that's how she found out about it. The last time she was happy was in the late 60s when she'd gotten married, Sarah offered, so maybe she kept dressing that way so the feeling would stay. It made a sort of sense to me: her smile was the thin-lipped, cheerful smile of a betrayed woman stuck forever in a Christian split-level in the Midwest. Over the years she stayed with him and seemingly never said a word, just walked around wearing that out-of-date *Laugh-In* costume, hoping that love would loop back and catch her on its wave. Kelli's mom was trapped in the uncanny valley.

———

In Japan, the annual ritual Hinamatsuri, or Doll Floating, happens on Girls' Day. A set of Hina dolls traditionally given to the family when the girl is born are displayed on a tiered platform decorated with peach flowers. The platform represents the levels of power within an imperial court: emperor, empress, attendants, etc. After the festival one puts away the dolls quickly; if they don't, the superstition goes, the girl will never be married. When the festival concludes families release dolls made of paper into a nearby river as a sort of exorcism. A child's bad luck or impurities can be transferred to the doll, legend goes, by breathing on it or rubbing it against yourself. The doll is then thrown into the water to be carried far away.

There is much to be said for the destruction of dolls as a symbolic exorcism. Think of all the Barbie dolls with their suddenly punk haircuts, all the legs broken off to reveal that one bare knob. Once in junior high I snuck out of my parents' house and met up with some friends on the playground of our old elementary school. It was the middle of the night and we built a meager bonfire with someone's Zippo and sipped cheap liquor and burned a couple of Barbies, the melted plastic distorting their faces from pert to dystopian. When the remnants of our revelry were found the next day by school staff, the school board was alerted. Some reportedly worried there were Satanists lurking in the subdivisions. Really we were just playing at rebelliousness, kids messing around, trying to destroy a symbol of the bad luck we'd been born into.

As with all things related to gender, the distinction between subversive and reifying is very slippery. Sort of like when Alice realizes the "Jabberwocky" poem is a looking glass poem and must be read backwards, but when she faces it toward the mirror, she experiences simply a different kind of confusion: the letters are recognizable, but the words are meaningless.

Cover the eyes of a Worlds of Wonder Talking Julie doll, and it says: *Can you see okay? It's kind of dark.*

When you uncover its eyes, it rewards you with a coo: *Ooh, it's getting brighter.*

MISSING FILE #1: WOOLLY RHINOCEROS / ANCIENT CAVITY TOOTH

In 1930 a writer referred to the woolly rhinoceros as a monster, and its suffocation inside a tar pit as a sealing up in the oily earth. Bringing the big body to the earth was a challenge met by a young team of soldiers from the Polish Army. The giant horns had been used in ritual display; the soldiers noted drawings on the vertebrae by the man who killed it, or his sons, or his sons or daughters. The omission of garments and a ridiculous head are indications the Paleolithic artist possessed great skill. In poetry, exaggeration and elision are prized; also alliteration. Animals were more precisely drawn than humans, but this was not due to lack of ability. See for example Robin Hood Cave Horse. See for example Pin Hole Cave Man. Men drew themselves crudely, as if they had never seen one another or as though trapped alone in the oily earth or as if their eyes prevented them from seeing the human form as object. By contrast, they carved animal likenesses precisely, and in the animal's own bone. They crouched for warmth, taking on the hunched shape of a stone inside the cave where later their own unremarkable blank bones would be found. For a long time, drawings were carvings. For a long time, carvings were done on bone and art was a side effect of hunting.

—

An exciting development: as the large ice sheets of Siberia thaw, well-preserved remains of giant prehistoric monsters will reveal themselves. Let us hope the paleontologists are alert with their tools. When the water trickles out of the bath, the bright-colored toys are scattered. I am already trying to clothe the child and warm the milk. I am "forward-thinking," a "multitasker," a good worker. Now we do not need to call soldiers to lift the massive bodies as we have sophisticated machines. We can lift the mammoth with only curiosity and propellers. Pin Hole Cave Man was found in 1928 by archaeologist A.L. Armstrong, who described the engraving as "a masked human figure in the act of dancing a ceremonial dance." He did not say why the figure was dancing, if he had just finished dinner, if he was making a house from the bones, if he made the house for his children, who gathered; if the man, tired as he was from his hunting, worked late into the night, scraping the keratin from the bloody horn and presented it to his daughter the next day as toy, as object of safety, sharp point, way to call for help.

———

The scientific name for the woolly rhino is Ancient Cavity Tooth, no, Coelodonta Antiquitatis, no, Commander in Chief, no, Stout, which means Extinct, which means Bog. The scientific name for the scientist is not Soldier, which means not Hunter but in between Scientist and Hunter. Like the soldiers who lifted the rhino to the earth and wrapped her in a receiving blanket and gifted her to the Polish Academy of Sciences. The scientist has no scientific name; in this he is like the Paleolithic artist. Today a person goes by many names, official, gendered, mated or otherwise.

The title of one article is "Siberia Surrenders Woolly Rhino Mysteries." It is not about the soldiers from Poland who, having cracked the heavy body from the ice, carried it like one great watery mass walking in concert, humming a popular song. This is about another woolly rhino, "a female that was unearthed near the mouth of a Siberian gold mine," which sounds not more than vaguely sexual.

Yesterday Russia began air strikes against Syria. Siberia is not Russia but it is not not Russia. The article's author did not mean Siberia as a nation-state. S/he meant the land: "Siberia is a major source of well-preserved remains, particularly as the long-frozen tundra surrenders carcasses as it thaws as a result of climate change."

———

Here the artist has made a place for you to encounter the woolly rhino. You may touch its nose. You may not feed it. It is a mummy; it has organs but they are sleeping. Here, please: _____

_____

_____

_____

To surrender is a way to say to give oneself. To give oneself is a way to say one's self can be gifted, like the hollowed out horn. To compare land to a woman is a cliché of the highest order. It is laziness punishable only by the death of the poem. To say a poem is like a body is to say one's self is a machine. To say a body is erasable is to say extinction is a temperate clicking.

And the howl is a hum, the wail a whirring. These are the wrong things to say. These are pretty things to say. And like that, with one hand on the glass and one gloved hand inside the mouth of the woolly rhino, you have done it.

MISSING FILE #2: DODO PARADISE, A FOUND TEXT

> "Only a few are left. It's up to you to make a plan for their survival. What would you do?"
>
> —www.dodobird.net

They say that they are dumb, but I think they are cool. But they are not alive. Long live the dodos! If we found more egg-sisted LOL we should keep them in a Special Island for Them to Live, a secret forest with a grill in the border, an organized place like the Bermuda triangle. Or, knowing extinction may be the result of a lack of safety, suck them up with a vacuum, spit them out in a remote location & make them breed. ROFL. No predators, only scientists. The Island would be named "Dodo Paradise." I would grow a bunch of them. Once I got the hang of it, I could pull it off. I would let no one go on the island.

I visit the island to see how they are doing. Hello dodo, I say. Long live the dodo. There is water all around the big island. We build a wall so they won't swim away, bye-bye dodo. I put posters everywhere: WHO WILL SAVE THE LIFE OF THIS DODO. If anyone goes to the island, unless I say so, jail for fifteen to twenty years. If anyone goes and makes a threat to kill one, jail for sixteen to twenty-three years. If anyone goes and KILLS one, I put them in jail for twenty to fifty years and kill them.

Dodo birds are epic. Treat them nice. They are not lab rats. To cement the Love of Dodo, train prospective "pet parents" in care and maintenance of baby dodos, in a brooder in a dodo coop. Study the dodo family. Draw them, write a book about them. :-) Run tests, know what happens in winter, spring, summer, and fall. Be so happy, creator of sanctuaries!

If I can't find an island, then everything I said above would never be true.

MISSING FILE #3: PANTHERA LEO LEO, OR, A CIVICS LESSON

A girl walks down the hallway in junior high wearing stone-washed jeans and a choker, assuming no one will touch her though many will look. As Aristotle writes, *The lion ... progress[es] by an amble; the action so called is when the animal never overpasses the right with the left but always follows close upon it.* This may appear artful but isn't, as a cat traverses the sill of an open window. The middle school has no walls, just folding accordion slats to divide classrooms into four blocks—*genera*—named for the colors of the school and its mascot. Gold Block. Black Block. The girl imagines her body losing a dimension, her self as a pocket door: a way to evade the predatory place altogether.

—

Aristotle's *History of Animals* is thorough; at times it is accidentally funny, as when he writes *Hedgehogs copulate erect, belly to belly* or notes that lions don't have under-eyelashes and piss backwards. Other times he states the obvious—e.g., *Furthermore, of animals some are horned and some are not so.* Is he being hubristic, thinking that because he is the only one to record, he is the only one to see, believing his account will survive the extinction of the thing itself? Or is he being pessimistic, assuming the horned / unhorned animals are temporary and therefore necessitate description? After all, sometimes the banal is transformed by annihilation into the marvelous.

Most likely Aristotle's tone reveals affectation of style, not spirit. Or Aristotle was simply so entranced with the act of describing that readers are to be swept out into the sea of his mind, as when a magician pulls the tablecloth, leaving behind a centerpiece still in place.

———

Spring afternoons the yellow buses line the cul-de-sac looking mean-spirited and institutional. White dogwood blooms shed onto the steps at the school entrance. I hate them: the moment they bloom, the boys start joking that they smell *just like pussy.*

That spring a girl has a seizure in our biology class, thrashes about on the floor like a fish on the speckled deck of a boat. The teacher kneels down and removes the girl's shoes, inexplicably. We'd been reading an article about extinction; the teacher, projecting images onto the gray cinderblock wall, had explained it as a process nearly done and nearly undone, many times over. *The last wild Atlas lion was killed by a French colonial hunter in 1922 in Morocco on Atlas mountain—that is, a mountain bearing the lion's own name.* Cut to grainy shot of heavy lion head, grasped by the mane by a grinning man with a predictably wide stance. The author added with anemic wit: *The history books may have left a chapter or two out of the story.*

Later that day one of the boys—maybe emboldened by the sight of the epileptic girl in a moment of biological abandon—grabs my friend by the dogwood and shoves her against a wall. He bares his teeth at her, says, *Ooh. Ooh I like that.*

———

Extinction is a very old book, sliced open and re-sealed over and over. In writing a report on extinction, one must note multiple names used for a single species: for instance, the Atlas lion may be called the Barbary lion, Moroccan Royal lion, or *Panthera leo leo.* You must record the killings of all three to know whether the species is truly a goner.

Extinction is a symphony of killings in different time signatures. In the Roman Empire, the state imported Barbary lions from North Africa for gladiator games and baiting, where a lion battles a pack of dogs, encircled by drunk human spectators. Lion baiting was a blood sport with a long run: King James I of England kept his lions in the Tower, a floor above the traitors and heretics, because it was fun to watch lions tear apart dogs like toys, or at least as fun as sitting around identifying witches, his other pastime. But he let his polar bear amble into the Thames on a long silver chain to hunt for fish all on its own.

Sometimes I think of naming as a paternal act: Adam sits, petting his little zoo. Other times I think it is a statement of disbelief, a lack of faith; a worry that if we don't have a word for something, it won't let us hold it anymore.

—

Journalism, fourth period. I sit at my green melamine desk and record the objects in the room: "The yellow ribbed border paper is torn slightly in the left corner. Below it is a faint chalk mark, roughly an inch in length," etc. I do not write about Shelley, her satin jacket, skunk mane of black hair, and thin black eyeliner, who has threatened to beat my ass at the trailer park across the street after school any day now. I do not write about the baseball-hat-wearing Christian girl who was my science partner and who recently shot herself, and do not write that I think it was because she loved girls or wanted to be a boy or both, I'm not sure. Nor do I write about the pockmarked Civics teacher who invites me to sit on his lap or to swim with him after school and counts aloud the days until his retirement at the start of each class.

Anyhow description does not involve, but is itself, a type of movement. The movement may be of an accidental or strategic kind; most often a combination, as when one describes their childhood while a little bit drunk at a party. More naming means more strategy, more accidents, more baiting. *Gold Block. Partner.*

I wonder where Shelley is now. She lives in my brain and sparkles with her violence.

———

In Critical Thinking, first period, 1993, we sit for a fifty-minute class in an open square space with plastic accordion walls the color of almonds. I sit near my friend who has gap teeth and reddish blond hair that makes her look a little wild and feline though she's no lion, just a breeze.

The teacher—male, early thirties—makes frequent use of an overhead projector. In a lesson on criteria, he uses a special red pen to outline qualities of the Perfect Woman: *a) green eyes b) blond hair* and *c) a curvaceous body weighing appx. 105 to 110 pounds.* I know what curvaceous means but some don't, so he adds in red marker *Big Breasts, Backside,* then has us look it up in a dictionary anyway. Finally, he demonstrates the limitations of criteria in critical thinking by explaining how a curvaceous waitress infected him with a painful sexually transmitted disease.

With these examples, he uses his young man's hands to wrap up us girls and place us outside the beige slatted city walls. We know what is happening. We wait there by the gate, looking at our clawed feet.

———

Aristotle says, *Many animals have memory, and are capable of instruction; but no other creature except man can recall the past at will.*

Aristotle says:

A) Man is by nature a political animal.
B) What separates humans from animals is rationality.
C) The city is a machine.
D) Machine.

Aristotle says the city is organic, which is like saying cruelty is organic. Or rather, it is like saying division of resources and power is organic, which is like saying cruelty is organic.

Erasing takes a long time: the rain of pink rubber shreds, the rubbery smell of it. The girl writes in her notebook: *Miss Royal Leo, Leo Royal Atlas*, drawing a lion with hearts for eyes, listing her favorite things about lions and gladiators.

She has been here a long time. Her position continues to be imperfect.

MISSING FILE #4: A FEW FACTS ABOUT BEES

Bees have two stomachs: one for eating, one for storage. Bees have undertakers who carry the dead and dying away from the hive. Bees suffer from "disappearing disease." In April a truck carrying hundreds of hives as freight glanced off a guardrail, flipped, and released fourteen million bees to the air. It had been traveling at speed through America's wettest city to a local blueberry farm which the honeybees were to pollinate for pennies on the dollar. A single worker bee makes 1/12 of a teaspoon of honey in his lifetime. When I was a child, I licked manuka honey off the spoon when sick. I yanked handfuls of honeysuckle from the neighbor's vine. I would pull the pistil out of the flower carefully to release what I had been told was honey, waving to the neighbor who owned seven exotic birds and had a pale, quiet daughter.

When the truck turned the bees loose, they scrambled, trying to find position, to signal the way like a compass. The driver wrapped his arms over his face, the reporters were stung until clusters of the bodies of bees littered the interstate. Together the neighbor girl and I would collect horse apples in the front yard and examine them carefully for caterpillars. We'd return at dusk to her house, with its one room just for the birds, carpeted in newspaper with branches anchored to the windows, extending all around.

"Disappearing disease" sounds both psychological and cultural, as if the bees, having come from ancient Egypt, watched Western postmodernity collapse and turned back to return to the pyramids. When faced with a predator, bees do the Wave: they flick their wings, arch their bodies, send a ripple across the comb. A queen is protected all winter. The workers huddle around her to keep the heat up. They rotate from the outer to inner ring so no one is left long out in the cold. Her whole life the workers feed her, bowing to release royal jelly from their head glands. The neighbor's red-nosed, jovial husband had a diminutive nickname and hung himself in the basement many years later, to everyone's surprise.

The bees swarm into the boxes. We organize the boxes and send the boxes into the gasoline atmosphere so they may do their tremble dances in the cool mist of an automatic sprinkler. But transportation is not predation. Is it.

MISSING FILE #5: THE ORTOLAN BUNTING

In 1996 former French President Francois Mitterand invited thirty guests to his last supper. One was delighted to attend and offer condolences, admittedly a delicate balancing act. President Mitterand sat mute at the head of the table, blankets wound around him, eyes glorious and blank as bicycle reflectors. In the corners were his bodyguards. At first he seemed to be sleeping, but with a sweeping blur of white linen—when the servants arrived with *the birdies*, the chef called them—the former President grinned, teeth shined in spit. The size of the birds was delightful, as if the very soul of France draped across a fig. A tiny dog no more efficiently arouses sympathy. The thirty guests and the dying President assumed what is called the "eating posture," draping napkins over their heads like brides, so as not to offend God for masticating the soul of France. At last spooning the birds into their mouths, biting into thirty hazelnut heads, the guests agreed it would have been a shame to waste what had been bound and drowned in Cognac. I would have peeked through my napkin. The President died seven days later having refused subsequent food, stuffed to the end with two small winged souls of France. The media was unrelenting. *Two!*

———

Some ornithologists translate birdsong into human language: to assist with memory, perhaps, feel they've bridged a divide or to make jokes. For example the ortolan song is known as *A little bit of bread and no cheese* which sounds like a child's rhyme, mice running from the carving knife, and makes me think of a dumbshow, because you could mime, easily, *A little bit of bread*, and even *no cheese*, the dissatisfaction with one's plate by waving your hands with a furrowed brow and exaggerated frown. Ortolan eggs are pearly and covered in veins, and the real song of the ortolan is here written, but that song is not a phrase but a series of ridiculous words. The ortolan nest is a kind of bowl made of horsehair and noisome weeds, according to John Clare, the great poet of birds and being poor. Inside the bowl, the eggs are sly, holding the pattern for next and next ortolans. I know one ornithologist who has the singing voice of a sexless ghost continent. Once I wrote to ask about the bird in *The Progress of Rhyme*. What is it? I asked. I had been comparing the birdsong in the poem to a mirror stage, where the poet sees how separate he is from the bird. His mastery sounds like this: *Wew-wew wew-wew, chur-chur chur-chur Woo-it woo-it … Tee-rew tee-rew tee-rew tee-rew Chew-rit chew-rit Will-will will-will grig-grig grig-grig.* The ornithologist wrote back: a nightingale. I believed him to be weary of citizens and their ignorance of birds.

———

The Mitterand affair increased the ortolan's value among poets. Everywhere I look there is another poem for the ortolan: behind the checkout counter at the deli, inside the mailbox, inside the cherry wood dresser of America's guilt. I myself have never understood the love of birds, which refuse to be held. Of the proliferation of ortolan poems, I worry. How will I sell my own poem on the ortolan? I feel betrayed by the little victims shut up in a box, by their magnetic needle bones. I begin to sympathize with the eater. Maybe it's not to want to be God to use what God gave you, not sinister nor hubristic to place the body in your mouth and pierce the head with your front teeth like a stapler. Surely deliciousness is not a thing your mother gives you before slapping you for what you are, a little beast made of hunger and curiosity. It is so like you—to forget what you are, just like an animal. Maybe the bird was a gray seducer of kings and emperors. Shut up in the box in the dark, consuming all the figs without stopping until the sticky seeds lined its intestines like diamonds. What if it doesn't see the dark bath coming but still accepts it, even loves it a little, the cage a little Moses basket. *Grig-grig.* What if that.

MISSING FILE #6: ELON & THE STARMAN

"Why Falcon Heavy & Starman? Life cannot just be about
solving one sad problem after another. There need to be things
that inspire you, that make you glad to wake up in the morning
and be part of humanity. That is why we did it.
We did it for you."

—Elon Musk, March 10, 2018, Twitter

Like a mother donning an oxygen mask, Elon first dresses himself:
a gray button-down, a shirttail hem. Then it's Starman's turn. It's
difficult to fit the white flame-resistant spacesuit, complete with
3D printed helmet and touchscreen-compatible gloves, around
the dummy. It's like lifting a damn mattress. Elon takes a break,
has a drink.

A spacecraft like his needs a ballast, or what some call a dummy
payload. Elon solicited ideas from Twitter and minutes later has his
answer when a stranger suggests Elon's own 2008 Tesla roadster
in midnight cherry be sent into space like a Dadaist readymade.

Now his staff carry Starman to the car like plodding pallbearers
and rest Starman's right hand on the steering wheel, left arm on
the sill. Starman is cool as a cucumber, a pocket full of bitcoin.
Onto the dash someone screws a Hot Wheels convertible with a
tiny Starman at the wheel: a toy on a toy on a toy, a punning matry-
oshka. A plaque bearing the names of employees who worked on
the project is screwed to the undercarriage, and a copy of *Hitchhiker's
Guide to the Galaxy* placed in the glovebox. The sound system loops
"Space Oddity." Elon smiles: he and the Roadster sure had some
good times together.

Goodbye friend. Cheers. *Clinkity-clink.*

Ten. Nine. Eight.

———

Starman goes on to travel 470 million miles around the sun, or nineteen light minutes from Earth, attached to a spaceship named the Falcon Heavy. It floats in the velvet estate that is space, that kingdom, that buyer's market. Once Elon had a spaceship named the Dragon after "Puff the Magic Dragon." The name was a slight to critics who thought SpaceX's mission was a fool's errand or a wild goose case, not what it is, which is the bright gold egg of a grand idea. Some people have no faith, when faith is handmaiden to innovation.

My son turns six the day a Dragon becomes the first American spacecraft in history to autonomously, or privately, dock with the International Space Station, making its way into its intergalactic garage at 6:02 a.m. At that time I am toasting waffles in a four-slice toaster, readying the children for school, climbing the stairs again and again. Repetitive work, as on the Tesla assembly line where a fine coating of silica coats the workers like stardust and where Red Bull energy drinks pile up in a shimmering mountain of pristine silver and blue, reflected in each worker's Tesla stare. This is according to a Tesla worker who was burned on the face and hands by liquid metal and says things can get very hectic and goes on and on about wolves.

Today the Falcon Heavy spaceship can be rented for $90 million (launch services purchased separately). It can carry 122.6 people of average weight, and you could be one of them. It is important to believe in possibility; believing in possibility allows you to bob on the surface of your own youthfulness. Believe you can come, that you can build a guest house and live there alone with your long face. SpaceX offers a modest discount for multiple trips: you know you'll want to come back. You probably left something on Earth.

———

Thailand. Young people are the future. Consider the soccer team: what a wet hollow they were in. Imagine being trapped in such alien darkness. But Elon reminds us that we are a global neighborhood, a worldwide Gotham. Elon is a noiseless and patient spider. He orders a liquid oxygen tube stripped from a spaceship and fashioned into a submarine; he names it Wild Boar in honor of the team, tests it in his pool and sends it straight East. Were it his own rib it would be no more precious.

That night Elon falls asleep imagining his bed is an inflatable rescue pod. He thinks of the Dragon carrying cargo though originally designed to carry seven humans of average weight. He dreams each child is a pea floating in an ocean, or is it a field, or a Bellagio fountain, a midwestern mall. *A life of ease. Every one of us has all we need.*

———

Ad Astra is the school Elon custom designed for his five sons. Anyone can complete an entry form, available free on the school website, because we are a country of weird opportunity. To apply, a child composes four essays in response to hypothetical scenarios, including "Goldilocks," which reads: "Humans are looking for a new home. They have eleven planets from which to choose: Sun, Baloo, Winnie, Grizzly, Polar, Smokey, Blue, Atlas, Panda, Yogi, or Kodiak. Consider the variables of safety, resources, growth potential. Determine the three best and three worst planets for humanity. Explain why."

At a party my son wants the birthday girl's balloon. It is lavender with white polka dots. He puts his hand around the ribbon, will not let go. I put my hand on his hand. I say no to him, as I do again and again. *No no no. That one is not yours. Another one is yours.* He screams this is the one he wants, but finally relents and takes the canary yellow one instead. We walk to the car, and he lets go, and it moves quickly up past the tree line over the houses while he screams and kneels to the grass, clutching his favor bag. One up, one down.

Another day, after school: Home Depot. I need to fix our leaking basement, kill the mice, stop up our leaky roof, seal the crackling lead paint on the windows. My son is bored, has eaten the apples and kicks me as I walk down the aisle, eyes drawn to the orange clearance stickers as though they were pollen and I an enterprising insect. He begins to type a story on my phone. It is called "The Five Dragons of the South." In it a young dragon runs from a giant monster. His father urges him to go to the spring. He writes: *But when they came to the spring there was a volcano. They walked very slow and the lava slid them over the gap where the spring was. Until the dragons had to battle and the dragons won. The end.*

———

Have you seen a child with his cheeks full of cherries, red juice around the mouth like a halo, bursting with talk. He cannot stop himself. *Watch this. Watch this. Are you watching. You are not watching. Do you want to play with me. I am not tired. I am not tired. Play with me.* My son takes his Matchbox cars and gives each one a driver which he attaches with a rubber band: a Lego man, a plastic leopard, a rabbit with a chewed ear. He shoots them across the living room. The cats run from these small weapons; cars slam into the baseboard, hard, chipping the paint. *Hurrah!*

Summer. We play a game in the car on the way to the zoo. The game is: list what you want, and add on in a round. I want: a vacation. A vacation and a dog. A vacation and a dog and a new rug. My son wants forty remote controlled pterodactyls. My son wants to be able to change into any animal and forty remote controlled pterodactyls. My three-year-old daughter wants ice cream. Ice cream and a robot with seventeen eyes. We laugh. But the drive is long, and my son insists on one remote controlled pterodactyl. Just one. He won't stop. He begins to cry, to scream. *I need one*, he says. *You mean you want one. Want and need are different.* I am wearing my mom voice, that heavy, stiff coat. Ancient and durable.

We want everything, don't we. A child, a dress, a goal, a mouthful of sweets. Athena with her goatskin shield fringed in snakes, her head of Medusa. The ghost limb to rejoin. It is our story of destruction, the story of salvation, a swinging door made of bird bones and Lily of the Valley. We want everything: a spring for Elon. An end. A win.

MISSING FILE #7: ALREADY WE ARE LESS THAN EVER BEFORE

Fereidoun M. Esfandiary hypothesized the sun was the heart of utopia. He changed his name to FM-2030 to mark the year he'd turn 100. Interviewed by Larry King, FM-2030 wears a heavy white robe and says his new name is "neat." Larry smiles indulgently. "Do you believe people will be named this way in the future?" FM-2030 says, "No. We will have the ability to change season. 2030 will be a magical time, a dream, a goal: we will be ageless. Everyone will have an excellent chance to live forever." FM-2030 must have felt especially disappointed when dying of pancreatic cancer so early, at sixty-nine. As for the sun—bountiful with free energy, FM-2030 said it would run machines, copy everything and ourselves, so we'd never run out of anything ever again. No more competition. We'd stop beating up on each other. Plus, synthetic organs would make death a relic. *Why swell'st thou? Death, thou shalt die,* etc. Larry King is fixated on the name, like a big gray bear hunched over a ball. "You are not saying by taking this name that we will be named this way. But we will have our heritage," Larry goes on, straightening his tie. "Already we are less hereditarian than ever before," replies FM-2030 in a subdued, heroic way.

———

Elsewhere FM-2030 said, "I am a twenty-first century person accidentally launched in the twentieth. I have a deep nostalgia for the future." He said the pancreas is a stupid, dumb, wretched organ.

More than 100 people have been cryopreserved since 1967, housed in metal cylinders full of liquid nitrogen in a warehouse. When a body is preserved—not just a brain—the patient is a "whole body member." With his new name, FM-2030 demonstrates how renaming is a form of discovery, the apprehension of a new identity or use for an existing thing. It's marvelous how a tongue, making a sound received by the ear, transforms in the mind a material, giving it a use well beyond its present existence. You know what I mean? Just, wow. Lately my son talks a lot about Getting Dead: "Actually I don't like this flavor lip balm. I'm giving it to you, to have for your whole life until you get dead!" At bedtime: "What was I going to ask? Oh. What happens when your life is done?" The books say: Offer nothing beyond the scope of the child's question. As if that's possible, as if every call and response weren't a widening circle.

In *The Prelude*, Wordsworth writes of a boy standing on a cliff, imitating the owls who respond in kind until the mountain and pool below become a mess of sounds, a tornado-in-a-bottle: the owl call, the hollow echo of the boy's call, rendering indistinguishable what is human or animal, echo or utterance. Or even what speech is anyhow. Wordsworth offers a metaphor: the idea of origin is the naivest—or possibly vainest—of human concepts. When I was a child, a friend with straw-like hair and the body of a translucent scarecrow told me how her aunt, a farmhand, died by falling into a silo. Echo. Echo. Echo.

———

A twenty-something woman tells her Reddit followers she has terminal cancer and asks for donations. The funds aren't for a cure, but to have her brain cryopreserved after death. She succeeds, though not enough to be a whole body member. Now her father records daily messages for her future/afterlife brain. They all begin the same: "Hello, honey …"

Incidentally, Mormons don't believe people get a planet populated with their own families after death, but they don't exactly refute it.

If that were true, my mother, father, brother, and I would be on our own planet with my mother's cousin Mary, a severe anorexic from the backwoods who once tried to kill her own mother by throwing piece after piece of hot fried chicken at her in a rage. The Reddit girl was engaged; her fiancé wondered if he should be frozen, too, eternally bound to his extraordinary ice girl in her super form. Today he is married to an organic woman and works for a conservative think tank.

———

Wordsworth's owls never appear to us or the boy. It's unclear whether the event—the eruption—happens at sundown, or sunset—the poet leaves it ambiguous. Determining what is the midpoint of day or night is a fool's errand anyway. What is clear is that the boy dies, ending up at the bottom of the lake below a shimmery surface reflecting the sky and *that uncertain heaven.*

Once I took my son to AquaTots Swim Club and tried to make him into a Goldfish. We circled together in the water while a big man we didn't know shouted at us enthusiastically, instructed me to dunk my son's head underwater and I did it because I thought it was good for him. What did I know. He emerged full of newfound courage, but when we left he was clutching a purple plastic dolphin that lights up underwater and begged never to return.

———

When I turn thirty-nine, my son gives me a card shaped like Frida Khalo and says, "It's Daylight Savings Time, you have a choice: you can turn either eleven or dead!" That night I see Patti Smith perform live with my Mormon friend Lisa. Patti shakes her hips and shoots the stink eye at anyone recording with an iPhone; Lisa and I toast our mules to *Horses.* As a kid, just reading the word *death* made my stomach flip-flop: the actual letters and my somatic recoil became nearly indistinguishable from its meaning. The *d* was the worst but the way *-eath* follows like a slack, wet sheet felt terrible and viral. A real sock in the chest. Now a mother, I imagine a children's book titled *Breaking the Bad News*. Table of Contents: Death: subsection, Cancer. Things that Eat People: Sharks, Bears, Other People. Capitalist Fictions: Linear Progress, Heaven. One day, after saying something so full of grace the words hang in the air as if made of filament, wisdom, and sugar, you'll trip over an electrical wire or something and fall flat on your face. You're an animal, not a god. Thirty-eight is not one of your choices.

Are you ready? I believe you are ready.

NOMEN NUDUM

> Had they made as good provision for their names as they
> have done for their relics, they had not so grossly erred in
> the art of perpetuation. But to subsist in bones, and be but
> pyramidally extant, is a fallacy in duration.
>
> —Sir Thomas Browne

Geologist Rev. William Buckland (1784-), of the Society for the Acclimatization of Animals, distinguished professor at Oxford University, spent his free time eating his way through the animal kingdom. Believing the stomach ruled the world because it could eat the world, he consumed sea slugs, earwigs, kangaroo, seal, porpoise, dog, and more. His voracious appetite was, it must be said, an inspiration: acquaintance John Ruskin, fellow jack of all trades—botanist, watercolorist—himself lamented missing one of Buckland's favorite snacks of grilled mice on toast. Because I feel close to him, and I want you to as well, from here on let us call him William.

At a dinner party in 1848, William and his fellow guests were shown what appeared to be a pumice stone in a silver casket, only to learn they were viewing the relic heart of Louis XIV of France, taken from the royal tomb by a scorned member of the family. The guests were the last to see it, for William announced *I have eaten many strange things, but I have never eaten the heart of a king!* before gobbling it up like so much dried jerky. Will was a geologist, but he was also a priest; perhaps the gesture was accompanied by a loosening of the clerical collar. This gives the scene an even more obviously subversive flair. Had William resisted eating the king's heart he could have studied it; so perhaps he says, in chewing and gulping it down to be dissolved in his intestine, something like: *knowledge is less than hunger*. Buckland's hunger as the apex of a Dionysian spin: *history is less than experience*. *Monarchy is less than death*.

———

One article about William reads: *he voraciously consumed knowledge as if it were the bread of life*. This is a simile made of two metaphors; it is redundant, as eating is redundant.

My first love and I once drove from Indiana to a cabin in Vermont. There I met a philosopher named George who said if, instead of eating, there was a pill to take that would provide all the nutrients necessary, he'd be the first to sign up. In his spare time, the philosopher sang country ballads with the voice of George Jones, and I desired him very much, though his lack of passion for gastronomy and seeming asexuality were surely related. Also I was painfully in love with his good friend. Too much appetite, I guess.

I think of the pill he says he'd take. I imagine it must be unlike any other pill in the world. Perhaps it could be shaped to look like food: a miniature egg, say, or a tiny apple.

A philosopher is unlike a geologist in important ways. If a geologist is an explorer, a cataloguer of the physical world, a philosopher regards the earth akin to how the elderly view meteorological science: they aren't sure it exists at all and would prefer to have conversations about the weather, to know if *your* weather is *their* weather. A geologist is unlike the poet, bobbing in an ocean of anticipatory nostalgia for the physical world despite paying taxes within it. The poet's body darting around like a little lost bird heart, fast and meaty. And the geologist is unlike the prostitute, who becomes unto herself a heroic virtuoso of the physical. A made-to-order thumb harp.

———

The discovery of an ancient animal skeleton can make a person feel suddenly proud in a parental kind of way, like the astronomer who names a star for his daughter and sees it as homage rather than absurd, if poignant, sentimentalism. You should know it was William who discovered the "Great Fossil Lizard," the very first material record of a non-avian dinosaur. The story of the discovery is for another time. In fact, he was to announce his discovery of the "Great Lizard," or "Megalosaurus," in a publication in 1822, but it failed to print. And so, for some time the "Great Fossil Lizard" had what is called in science a *nomen nudum*, a naked name, a scientific name given to an organism when the circumstances of the thing's discovery, and its given name, hasn't yet been published in print. In other words, the Megalosaurus was baptized but not yet confirmed.

Somewhere another doctor began talking about the bones himself, scooping William's discovery, so there was a race to name the thing like the race to the moon, or a race to *name* the moon—which seems a good metaphor for naming a dinosaur which is, after all, another terrifyingly large thing humans had never seen up close. Later another scientist named Ferdinand tried to christen the Great Lizard with a complete binomial: *megalosaurus conybeare*. But that is one *nomen oblitum*—a name to be forgotten, as scientists didn't much take to it. In science *nomen oblitum* means the name is not supposed to be used. I apologize. Please forget I used the forgotten name; remember only what the thing is called today, a name given in 1827: *Megalosaurus bucklandii.*

I offer you this anecdote by way of penance: when I was a girl, I went to a Christian summer camp called Camp Tecumseh located near Delphi, Indiana, on the Tippecanoe River. The girls in my cabin and I moved through woods to make it to chapel on Sundays, rows of wood benches set into a hillside by the lake, in front of a giant wooden cross. While there I made everyone call me Charlie. Charlie was a good sport. Charlie prayed nightly and woke at dawn to swim. Because of Camp Tecumseh, Margaret Atwood's "Death by Landscape" has always haunted me: the reluctant, small landscape paintings in the narrator's living room; the girl dropping from the cliff without a sound. Silent as Wordsworth's Lucy Gray who disappears—poof!—into a puff of snow while crossing a river. Girl vanishings are very quiet. *Nomen oblitum.*

—

My parents got engaged after one week of dates. On the first of those dates, my father got a flat tire and he exited the car in the Indiana heat, kicked the hubcap in frustration, and cursed. Still they made it to open mic night at a local bar where my father sang a Dylan song in his sly baritone and watched as my mother chatted with a man to her left. When answering his question about how his performance went, my mother said something affirmative, to which my father asked, pointedly, *How do you know*. My mother felt this irritability, quickness to anger, jealousy, made him legible. He was not, as she would later tell it, a game player. *He is*, she would say with equal parts resignation and self-congratulation, *what he is*, a man of the type she recognized, a man static as asphalt. When they married, my mother erased her middle name, which had been her mother's name, Marie, to make space for her maiden name. She traded her mother for her father, or rather, traded her mother's name to ensure her father's would stay, on documents and such.

My mother's sentimental attachment is understandable: her father had died of a stroke when she was nineteen. He was working in the pharmacy he ran when a strong headache suddenly came on. Excusing himself, this man—Charles, a man I never met, who would not properly be called a grandfather—walked into his office, pausing to pick up the *Encyclopedia Britannica*, which he had been reading in fits and starts that year. His death was sudden as a snapping of the fingers. Surrounded by white porcelain jars full of gelatin capsules, powders of varied granulation, and apothecary jars scrawled with gold enamel script, the youngish tall man wearing glasses dropped. The man who liked science. A man who played the trumpet.

———

In 1823, having been told his neighbors had stumbled on some unusually large bones, William began a dig at Goat's Hole Cave, a limestone cave in south Wales. It is not known whether Buckland carried on this expedition, as he usually did, a large blue pouch that held mammoth teeth, skin, feces, a hyena skull. Portraits of the time show the pouch to be more of a sack, hung jauntily from a belt loop. While there, William indeed found a mammoth skull. More startlingly, nestled nearby were pieces of a human skeleton that had been soaked in red ochre, a pigment found in Tuscan clay. Where a pocket might have once been, William found a handful of periwinkle shells; around the waist, a belt of small rods made of mammoth bone. Around its neck was a necklace of perforated seashells. The red bones lay there under the dry earth, scattered like matchsticks.

William was sure, along with many other Reverends then and now, that before Noah's flood there was—at least as far as humanity is concerned—nothingness. This belief, alongside the jewelry, led William to declare he'd uncovered the burial site of a Roman prostitute or witch. The latter seemed more likely due to the presence of another animal bone—a sheep's shoulder blade—buried with the body, a particular type of bone once thought to have magical powers. William named the skeleton the Red Lady of Paviland, writing jocularly that the discovery of sheep shoulder would "afford ample matter to a Romance to be entitled the Red Woman or the Witch of Paviland."

If William was a cutup, the Red Lady was a shape-shifter, hard to pin down. At first sight, William thought the body might be that of an early tax collector, killed by a disgruntled debtor. But the body was also, as he would later write, very thin and tall, "as a witch should be." Friends suggested to William that "[his] enchantress" may have aroused the men in the area to "warlike deeds," that the mammoth bone rods were not part of a belt but pieces of a crude chess or backgammon-type game, and the yellowish shells kept in her pocket simply because they were beautiful. Because as William would note in a lecture before the British Archaeological Society, of which he was a member, "even among the uncivilized races, the female part of our species ... [is] anxious to decorate themselves with beads." She shifted shape many more times in William's mind. She was a loose woman, a prostitute; she ran a sort of gambler's casino out of her sorceress's cave. She may have even been, he quipped, Eve herself, which would explain her red color: "for it is not extraordinary when Adam was made of [red earth], that his rib should have a tinge of ruddle."

———

Let us imagine William carries her from the cave like a clackity bride. Meanwhile Mrs. Buckland—Mary, née Morland—gave their sons instruction on geography using globes she had made out of paper, colored, and inflated. She was secretly a scientist, but her mind had to be phrased differently because her husband disapproved. Her son Frank later said she was 'particularly clever and neat in mending broken fossils.'" Many of Mary's reconstructions are now preserved at the Oxford University Museum of Natural History, filed under the name *Buckland*.

When I was in middle school, all the girls wore Wet n Wild 501 lipstick. It wasn't red but purple, the color of a dangerous bruise, and this was how we signaled we were not whores but witches.

—

Once in college I overheard a docent at the Chicago Museum of Modern Art explain to a group of children that x-rays revealed Picasso's *Old Man with a Guitar* was painted onto a canvas originally painted with the figure of a woman. One could, she explained, just barely make out the woman's hip with the naked eye. Though the hip is literally painted under the man's leg, it appears she is sitting on his lap. Flirt. It felt as though the docent was uncovering two things at once: the woman beneath the man, and therefore also the falsehood of the man's apparent loneliness. Because the painting was begun and completed during Picasso's Blue Period, it is likely the woman was a prostitute. He painted during this time prostitutes, beggars, and drunks, in varied shades of blue, famously sinking into a depression worsened by the fact that no one wanted to buy his sad paintings of poor people, leaving him, tautologically, poor and sadder.

The Red Lady's body had been wrapped in fabric dyed with red ochre, a wet iron oxide. The painstaking procurement of red ochre for the dye is described by the fifteenth century painter Cennino Cennini. Having hunted and dug for it in the mountains of Tuscany—he describes the red pigment running through the land *like a scar on a face*—he used his horse-hair-tipped brushes to paint images of flesh, buildings, draperies. It's easier to excavate metal and grind it into pigment—*you actually cannot grind too much*, Cennini says—than to identify a skeleton and lift the puzzle pieces from the earth without eradicating evidence, which is, as we surely know by now, a kind of story. In the Renaissance the ochre color painters used varied according to the local soil; some regions had a pinkish tint, others a Siena red.

To take iron which is there, and make it into art, which records what happens, or what could have happened, or what was dreamt of or wished for or what was burdened. To take the earth which is there and make it into faith, which records what was dreamt of. To burden the earth *with* the faith.

———

A portrait of William in Westminster Abbey shows him holding a hyena skull. He wears a large black robe and smiles, looking out at something to the right. The background is black. He cradles the skull, his round pink face floating happily in the darkness. It is said William would race down the aisles of a lecture hall dressed like a Franciscan preacher, shoving a hyena skull in the faces of terrified undergraduates. He would shout repeatedly, "What rules the world?" until someone offered an answer. One student describes answering, "Haven't an idea," to which William replied, "The stomach, sir, rules the world. The great ones eat the less, the less the lesser still!"

I have never held an animal skull that I can offhand recall, though it seems a thing I've likely done. My brother and I once got lost in the Hoosier National Forest after smoking some pot and feared we'd not make it out by night. The color of the sky was like that of an invitation, opening to reveal a dark gold sheen. The fall leaves were in some places nearly up to our knees, as though we were wading through a burning lake. Eventually I was delighted to find one small deer antler for my trouble.

Today I display it on my fireplace mantle. It sprouts like a fat, hard branch from a vase of the same ivory color. Occasionally my son takes it down and jabs it menacingly at his sister.

———

In the 1950s some lab tech, assisted by carbon dating technology, read the Red Lady of Paviland's bone protein like a primer and found it was 20 percent fish, part woolly rhinoceros, part reindeer, and all male—not a Red Lady at all. For this error, perhaps Buckland should be forgiven. He became confused: the bones had been dyed in red ochre. They looked to him like food, like something to consume. Or perhaps he should not: he had not examined the skeleton before declaring it that of a woman. It was the ivory bracelets that convinced him, allowing him to make jokes about the ancient British witch to his colleagues at the Royal Society of London.

I feel sad imagining the world's anxiety over water and ice, and the female body, the belief that it speaks only in symbols, meaning it speaks without argument, is made simply of ovaries, periwinkle, spit, antiquity. In this way, the female body is like the *afikomen*, and maybe this is why Adam only slept once, when God forced it upon him so he could create woman. Eve: present yet undiscovered. Fragile yet foundational. Most consumable when consumptive. Most ideally, a delicious unknown.

Yet: not knowing in what *way* you mean consumable gets in the way of knowing, of knowing what you are, of how you may be incorporated. The *Oxford English Dictionary* gives three meanings. A) adjective: Of a foodstuff: suitable for consumption, edible. B) Able to be destroyed, esp. by fire; combustible. C) As a noun: A commodity that is intended to be used up or worn out by use. Cross-referenced with adj. *durable.* One might say it is a *Choose Your Own Adventure* piece. A love poem—no, an ars poetica—to the *OED* itself. Or: names are humiliating. The great ones name the less; the less, the lesser still.

Afikomen: a word originating with the Greek *epikomen*, meaning "that which comes after."

———

Technological revelation is sometimes simply the uncovering of error, and the scientist doffs his hat. But now with technology we can see the world. For example, the budget restricted cannot visit Paviland Cave in the flesh. Fortunately, you can now take a virtual helicopter tour on YouTube, with a soundtrack ("We Didn't Start the Fire" and "In the Middle of the Night" by Billy Joel). And if you search "Goat's Hole Cave," you find a GoPro video of a man carrying his redheaded daughter, about four, on an expedition to the cave. It is a remarkable film, both pedestrian and aesthetically disorienting; the film is sped up and accompanied by a metal soundtrack. The man begins by putting the girl on his back. He climbs over several miles of stone and ocean, and for a while, the viewer only sees the shadow of the man, daughter on his back, the sharp sunlight. The girl wears a hat that looks like a monkey's face; she has a navy spotted dress. He stops, pulls a fish from the water, and shows it to her and the viewer. The video is sped up; they climb farther. He puts her down. She sits like a doll, legs straight out, orange hair blowing straight up with the wind. He picks her up. When they enter the cave, we see the crevice entrance and the shadow of his head and baseball cap. Every opening looks like a cavity or an eye, a nose, a rejecting ghost. The drums beat louder, the guitar moves into a shamanic repetition. They disappear.

My son makes sense of death like this: the body of a person is chewed by animals or swallowed into a shallow belly of earth, so they become and become and become, always becoming. Never dissolved. At night his body becomes very hot, his feet twitch, and he explains to me how, in death, he will fold up inside a scarlet macaw, and we will meet somehow in our new jungle.

Two mouse feet lying still on little bread beds.

———

William would become more skilled, learning that there are delicate excavations and excavations akin to lobbing a porcelain dish at a wall, that there can be an art to digging. And that there was much before the flood. He became, in fact, author of *Evidence of the Flood*, arguing it is irrelevant whether one called it a flood or a glacier: the water simply wiped out everything before.

When people describe having always felt one sex or another, assigned or not, or attraction to one sex or another, straight or not, I cannot help but feel disappointed. The rhetoric of sustained identity is the cause of so much trouble. Are they not the same? Does one not make the other? Does land not shift just as dispassionately as the human form?

———

The Red Lady's bones are now a museum display. S/he has been transformed from waiting-to-be-discovered to a patchwork skeleton worth celebrating, a diva of sorts, a reality show winner. The curators have arranged the bones on a glass table, and a projector shines down like the sun, projecting in our mind's eye the image of flesh. S/he is like Snow White or a crime outline, or Alexander McQueen's best work, except she is 30,000 years old and the Real Thing. S/he has real bones instead of a gown that makes a woman look like a bird, a dancer, or—irony—a skeleton.

Gentlepersons, the Red Lady of Paviland, the first human fossil found in what appears to be the oldest ceremonial burial in all of western Europe—the tinny voice chimes eternally from the speaker, inviting intentional mishearing: *gentle purse on. Thread laid eve … the first hue man …*

As I typed *ars* in *ars poetica*, just now, sitting by this fire, Word auto-corrected it to *Mrs.* And then: *are.* And then: *art.*

———

Sometimes a scholar names a thing, and it falls under the waves of time and is worn smooth like a stone until it no longer appears a discovery. Then a new scholar names the same original thing, and it is suddenly new again, like an excavation of discourse. Imagine archeological excavation, the grand existential vertigo, discovery having been stretched across tens of thousands of years. And reassuring, maybe; one can become very tired of oneself and one's contemporaries. Thinking about this is like thinking about the holes in Francis Bacon's paintings, which can never be discovered, and that is all right because they are terrifying.

Recently I began to paint. I bought tubes of acrylic paints from the Michaels in town. I bought canvases and paper and a used easel and a drafting table that stood in the corner of the office unused and discerning. I painted women's faces, very large and very fast, as a child learning guitar bangs out chords. I found pictures of women everywhere; on book covers, in bookstores, magazines. I gave them green colors. And then one day a friend visited, and I showed her the paintings, both sheepish and proud. You have always painted, she told me. I didn't recall. Before you left Missouri, you gave me a painting of a vase of flowers. I didn't recall. It is still hanging in my house, she said. I said, *Well! What do you know. Here are some sad-looking women.*

To pry something out of someone, the meat of a walnut from its enamel-like shell, is an excavation—to uncover a lie, an infidelity. When confronted with the impossibility of knowing anything, I feel like an engine that won't turn over. It makes one face the exhausting knowledge one carries about oneself like a carapace, and I begin to feel very tired and want to stop moving.

To unearth identity is an excavation of the delicate type. The Red Lady's identity was there, until, in being "discovered," it was buried into Buckland's want.

———

The Roman word for brothel is *lupanar*, meaning a wolf den. A prostitute was called a *lupa* ("she-wolf"), as a girl is a Red Riding Hood, a wolf a becoming father; a she-wolf a fathering forth of lust; a warrior, a devil. Roman women used to dip lead-coated combs in vinegar and carry them through their hair so the salts would deepen their color. How heavy that must be: heavy as a petticoat, whalebone, chastity belt, as the discovery of one of the world's oldest ceremonial burials.

Graffiti in Pompeii found in 1824: "Let everyone in love come and see. I want to break Venus' ribs with a club and cripple the goddess' loins. If she can strike through my soft chest, then why can't I smash her head in with a club?" LOL.

When analyzing the sketches of large game found in ancient cave systems, scholars have determined that some scrapes and dents in the stone surface indicate that the paintings were attacked, *possibly in the belief that harming the image would wound a real-life animal.*

———

I feel aware that I have not brought these threads together. I have been an inefficient spider. I have made for you, as I wished, a museum of the Red Lady. Sometimes I pretend to be William, and he speaks like a professor: *I, like all men of science, know the body because of women and criminals; it was the dissection of these that founded modern medicine and gave us the ecstatic illustrations in Vesalius's De Humani Corporis Fabrica.*

After the flood, Noah sent out a raven and a dove into the wildness. The raven circled, it is said, until the water was dry. The dove was sent for confirmation that the water had receded. For centuries religious scholars have puzzled over the symbolism, and most especially, the sequence. Why the raven first? *Raven* may mean death; *dove* may mean peace. *Raven* may mean storm, or deliciousness, or the child's delight in destruction. *Dove* may mean storms, or deliciousness, or the child's delight in destruction. *Wildness* may mean that which is untouched by civilization, by humanity; that which is estimable only by other animals.

In Vesalius's anatomy treatise, the dissected bodies stand in fields and throw their discuses at the sun like superheroes. Though flayed from top to bottom and inaccurate, they are triumphant; the discus hovers over the earth like the dove holding the olive branch in its mouth.

Sometimes I pretend to be William, and he speaks like a lover: *my love, my red love, my Achilles of petticoats*. I listen to myself-as-William and throw up my hands in ecstasy at the unknowing, the elegant misnomers, until William and I become the dove, the raven, the water: all of it, returning home to Ararat.

NOTES

NICE WANTON

Lars and the Real Girl. Beverly Hills, Calif: 20th Century Fox Home Entertainment, 2008.

Dolls. Beverly Hills, CA: Empire Pictures. 1987.

Overboard. Beverly Hills, CA: MGM, 1987.

Bettelheim, Bruno. *The Uses of Enchantment: The Importance of Fairy Tales.* New York: Vintage, 1989. Print.

References to dildoll, the play *Nice Wanton or A pretie Enterlude called Nice Wanton* (1565, London, author unknown), *Adollizing; or, A Lively Picture of A doll-Worship: A Poem in Five Cantos* (1748), taken from Williams, Gordon. *A Dictionary of Sexual Language and Imagery in Shakespearean and Stuart Literature.* London: Athlone Press, 1991. Print.

Darwin Correspondence Project, University of Cambridge. https://www.darwinproject.ac.uk/people/about-darwin/family-life/darwin-s-observations-his-children. Web. Accessed 6.5.20.

Idov, Michael. "Meet the Human Barbie." GQ. July 12, 2017. https://www.gq.com/story/valeria-lukyanova-human-barbie-doll. Web. Accessed June 2020.

MISSING FILE #1: WOOLLY RHINOCEROS / ANCIENT CAVITY TOOTH

Ed. Paul Pettitt, Paul Bahn, and Sergio Ripoll. *Palaeolithic Cave Art at Creswell Crags in European Context.* London: Oxford University Press, 2007. Print.

Heil, Andy. "Siberia Surrenders Woolly Rhino Mysteries." December 6, 2012. https://www.rferl.org/a/russia-zoology-wolly-rhinoceros-boeskorov/24791250.html. Web. Accessed 6.5.20.

MISSING FILE #2: DODO PARADISE, A FOUND TEXT

The entire text is taken, slightly edited, and rearranged from the website www.dodobird.net. These are the public's answers to the question posed on the website: "It's true, the Dodo Bird has been extinct for hundreds of years. But imagine a world where they are still alive, but only a few left. It's up to you to make a plan for their survival. What would you do?"

MISSING FILE #3: PANTHERA LEO LEO, OR, A CIVICS LESSON

Aristotle. *History of Animals in Ten Books.* London., H.G. Bohn, 1862. Print.

MISSING FILE #5: THE ORTOLAN BUNTING

Clare, John. The Progress of Rhyme. *John Clare, Major Works.* Ed. Eric Robinson and David Paulin. Oxford: Oxford University Press, 1984. Print.

MISSING FILE #6: ELON & THE STARMAN

Ad Astra: https://adastra.school

Evans, Will and Alyssa Jeong Perry. *MIT Technology Review.* "Tesla says its factory is safer—but it left injuries off the books." April 16, 2018. https://www .technologyreview.com/2018/04/16/143870/tesla-says-its-factory-is-saferbut-it-left -injuries-off-the-books/ Web. Accessed 6.7.20.

MISSING FILE #7: ALREADY WE ARE LESS THAN EVER BEFORE

"Larry King Interviews Transhumanist FM-2030." https://www.youtube.com/watch? v=XkMVzEft7Og. Web. Accessed 6.7.20.

Wordsworth, William. *The Prelude: 1799, 1805, 1850.* Ed. Jonathan Wordsworth, M.H. Abrams, and Stephen Gill. Norton Critical Edition, 1979. Print.

NOMEN NUDUM

Browne, Thomas. "Thoughts on Death and Immortality" (1605) as reprinted in Chambers's *Cyclopædia of English Literature*, 4th ed., Vol. 1 (1894): 432. Print.

Burd, Van Akin. "Ruskin and His 'Good Master,' William Buckland." *Victorian Literature and Culture* 36.2 (2008): 299-315. Print.

De Long, William. "The Story of The Zoologist Who Ate Everything—Including A King's Heart." December 22, 2017. https://allthatsinteresting.com/william-buckland. Web. Accessed 6.5.20.

Gordon, Elizabeth Oke. *The Life and Correspondence of William Buckland, D.D., F.R.S.* John Murray (London) 1894: 288. Print.

Graffiti in Pompeii: Harvey, Brian K. *Daily Life in Ancient Rome: A Sourcebook.* Cambridge: Hackett Publishing Company, Inc., 2016. Print.

Kölbl-Ebert, Martina. "Mary Buckland (Nee Morland), 1797–1857." *Earth Sciences History* 16. 1 (1997): 33-38. Print.

"afford ample matter to a Romance to be entitled the Red Woman or the Witch of Paviland: Sommer, Marianne. "'An Amusing Account of a Cave in Wales': William Buckland (1784-1856) and the Red Lady of Paviland." *The British Journal for the History of Science* Vol. 37.1 (2004): 53-74. Print.

ACKNOWLEDGMENTS

Pieces from this chapbook originally appeared in the following journals:

Missing File #1: Woolly Rhinoceros / Ancient Cavity Tooth	*A Public Space*
Missing File #2: Dodo Paradise, A Found Text	*Sonora Review*
Missing File #3: Panthera Leo Leo, Or, a Civics Lesson	*Broad Street*
Missing File #4: A Few Facts about Bees	*Black Warrior Review*
Missing File #5: The Ortolan Bunting	*Black Warrior Review*
Missing File #7: Already We Are Less Than Ever Before	*Proximity Magazine*

I must first thank my son Samuel, whose passion for animals and existential musings at a young age became the lifeblood of many of these essays. My daughter Anita's humor and lightness kept me buoyant and inspired throughout, and I am deeply grateful to her. Above all I owe this collection to my husband Alex, whose steadfast support and friendship has kept me creatively awake over the years.

I am also grateful for the support of my family, Aaron, Elizabeth, Frona, Maya, and Ron Powell, Kate Jamison, and Grace and Philip Hamilton; and friends Joanie Lipson Freed; Jessica Garratt; Arthur Getman; Rachel Gurstein; Katie Hartsock; Susan McCarty; Alix Olson; Emily Raabe; Dave Shaerf; Elizabeth Shesko; Lisa Wolf Smith; Erin Dwyer and Roger Wyn; and Julie Lambert and David Lambert, whose haunting photograph graces the cover. Thank you all, especially my Michigan friends, for making me feel at home.

Photo: Lisa Wolf Smith

Alison Powell's lyric essays have recently appeared or are forthcoming in *A Public Space*, *Black Warrior Review*, *Broad Street*, *Hayden's Ferry Review*, *Sonora Review*, and *Proximity Magazine*; recent poetry appears or is forthcoming in *Alaska Quarterly Review*, *Boston Review*, *Copper Nickel*, *Crazyhorse*, *jubilat*, *New Ohio Review*, *Prairie Schooner*, and more. Her book of poems, *On the Desire to Levitate*, won the Hollis Summers Poetry Prize and was published by Ohio University Press in 2014.

Powell's work has been supported by fellowships from Virginia Center for the Creative Arts, Vermont Studio Center, and the Crosshatch Center for Art and Ecology, and she has received awards from the *Greensboro Review*, *Proximity Magazine*, Fine Arts Work Center in Provincetown, and more. Originally from Indiana, she completed her PhD in English at the CUNY Graduate Center with a specialization in the Romantic poets. She is now Associate Professor of Creative Writing at Oakland University and lives with her husband, son, and daughter in Metro Detroit.